DEDICATION

I would like to dedicate this book of short stories to my family for all their help and support.

To my daughter, Miranda, and son-in-law, Jon, because they are the parents of the three main characters.

To my daughter-in-law, Sarah, for her help with the illustrations.

To my grandson, Conner, for the unique name of Henry Pancake.

To my son, Robert, so he doesn't feel left out!

Thank You!

INTRO

A DAY IN THE LIFE OF HENRY PANCAKE

This is a collection of 16 humorous short stories that are told by the main character, Henry Pancake. He is a senior Pug dog, who lives in the Upper Peninsula of Michigan.

Henry Pancake will introduce you to other canine family members and a few wild critters he meets in his daily adventures. I hope you enjoy reading these stories as much as I enjoyed writing them.

Henry Pancake

Greetings from
Michigan!

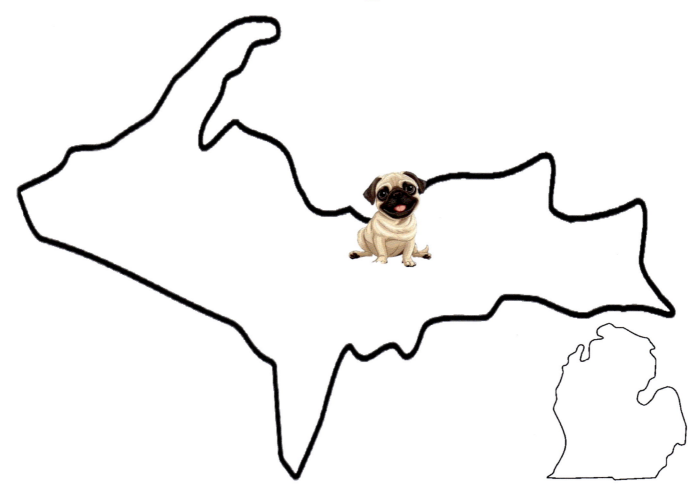

A Day in the Life of Henry Pancake

Please let me introduce myself…..I am Henry Pancake. I am an 11-year-old Pug dog. Most folks see me as a senior dog, but I prefer to see myself as a handsome, overgrown pup. In my eyes, I am still the young, handsome pup who came to live in Michigan's Upper Peninsula 11 years ago. For years I was the only pup, just me and my mom. I was living large, for a small dog. Then mom got married and it was the 3 of us. Life was good! Next came my new sister, Harley Bean. She's a pug like me, but not nearly as handsome or well behaved. She is both younger and smaller than I am, but she has an attitude twice her size. She is 6 years old now, and thinks she rules the roost (and she pretty much does). Life was good as an only pup, but HB is tolerable. I adjusted to life with my sister, then, along comes Ranger D. We now have a new brother (oh brother). He may be the youngest, but he's not the smallest. He's a chocolate Lab living with 2 pug dogs. He's almost 2 years old now. He's lanky and a bit goofy, but he's ours, so we'll keep him. I actually prefer spending time with Rangie more than the Bean. He's more of a big doofus and doesn't boss me around.

Almost every Saturday, Dad goes for a ride and takes Ranger D. with him. It gives Rangie a break from us and us a break from him. It works! Then, to my surprise, this special Saturday comes along and I am picked to go for a ride. Mom came with and the 3 of us headed out for the day. I had flashbacks to being the only pup. We drove for a long time, and then stopped at a grocery store. It may not sound like a fun day, but I sure felt special. After shopping is when the real fun begins. We went to my cousin's house. Turns out I have 3 cousins…an American Bulldog (Titan), an Old English Bulldog (Ellie) and a Boxer (Daisy). They are all quite large and a little scary. I'm not sure I even came up to their knees. I was afraid at first, but after we took turns smelling each other, we decided we were family and got along good. All that fresh air and running around was great. It was a new yard to explore with cool smells and so much more than I ever saw in my 11 years. Can you believe there were birds there that are bigger than me? I kid you not! I think they called them chickens, ducks and turkeys. They all had names, but my pug brain can't remember them all. There was also another pug dog there. He is 9 years old and his name is Frankie Doodle. I'm not sure, but I think he's my uncle. He's a little on the chubby side and didn't do too much running around. He mostly just laid around wheezing loudly. Except for the wheezing, he's very similar to a cement block.

I think the main reason for this visit was because of something called a cookout. My definition of a cookout is that the humans eat and the pups watch. What a fun day! I had so much fun with my humans and cousins, but the best part was that Harley Bean and Ranger D. had to stay home. I know this sounds snobby and that's not like me at all, but a day out and being the only pup, is priceless. So much excitement is exhausting for a pug, but I will remember it always. I can't wait to get home and fill in Rangie and HB all about this wonderful day in the life of Henry Pancake. The long ride home is very relaxingzzzzzz.

Henry Pancake goes to Jail

Henry Pancake here with an adventure I hope to never have again.
It all started as a normal day with Harley Bean and Ranger D. The 3 of us were playing keep away with a toy, when HB (the little stinker) really took it away from us. Mom was mad at her for spoiling our fun so Rangie and I got to go outside and play but she had to stay in.

Rangie's a lot bigger than I am, but I tried my best to keep up with him. He would bounce from one thing to another, while I stopped to take a rest. To my surprise, a little bunny hopped up and was checking me out. He had the biggest ears I've ever seen. His little nose twitched at me, and I'm sure I saw him wink (maybe not). His tail amazed me. It was just the cutest thing I've ever seen. I thought my tail was cute being all curled up, but his was round and fluffy like a big powder puff. I moved towards him and he hopped away. That's when Ranger D. noticed him. Yikes, off they went running so fast. Rangie was almost able to catch the puffy tail. I tried to keep up, but lost sight of them quickly. I had to stop for another rest, and realized I was lost.

I've never mentioned this before, but I am hearing impaired, or as Mom puts it "deaf". I walked around for a little trying to remember my way home, but no luck. I'm sure Mom was calling me, but I couldn't hear her. I wandered until I came to a road. There a car stopped and a nice lady picked me up. I'm not too good at reading lips, but I think she asked me where I came from. Since I couldn't answer, she brought me to jail (the local animal shelter). They made sure I had food, water and a blanket to lay on in my cell. Lucky for me, I have a chip in me that tells them who I belong to, so the Shelter could call Mom to come pick me up. It seemed like forever behind bars, and finally I heard a familiar bark. Mom, Dad, Rangie and HB all came to get me out of jail. They all seemed glad to see me, but not nearly as glad as I was to see them. Rangie kept licking me all the way home. I think it's his way of saying he was sorry for not watching me closer. Once home, I had to have a bath. Clean Jammie's and a treat before bed. I'll try never to leave the yard again. Prison changes a pug.

Happy, Happy, Happy
Easter
 (From the 3 of us)

Henry Pancakes Celebrates Easter

Henry Pancake here about to celebrate Easter. Mom and dad left the house early today to go to Easter mass at their parish, so we pups got to sleep in. We always have company over on Easter Sunday, so mom cooks a bunch of food. I'm not a fan of the sweet potatoes, but the ham is yummy!

Today mom and dad went outside without us. That doesn't happen very often, and we were quite puzzled by their behavior. When they came back in, they were laughing and seemed excited about something. They finally took us outside and the yard looked strange. They had it divided into 3 sections that were separated by a short fence. We could easily jump the fence, but figured they put it there for a reason.

Sure enough, Ranger D., Harley Bean and I each had our own section of the yard. It was easy to see that there were surprises laying in each section. I think this is the puppy version of an Easter egg hunt. So off I went, foraging for goodies. I found a new harness with my name and phone number on it, a pretty blue leash (my old one was getting a little frayed), a bouncy ball, a frisbee, a couple of rubber chew bones, and what's this? I see something else in the grass. As I run over to check it out, I see it's a doggy toothbrush. No way do I want this in my future. I quickly picked it up and brought it over to the Bean's section. I dropped it over the fence and no one even noticed. Next, I found a real bacon treat, which I ate immediately. Finally, I spotted one more object. A closer look showed me that it was toothpaste to go with the brush. Another trip to the Bean's section, and I am done foraging.

Mom and dad looked over all the loot we found. I could tell mom was surprised that Harley Bean had 2 toothbrushes and paste, when I didn't get any. I guess even the Easter Bunny can make a mistake (wink). Rangie is such a goof. The first thing he found was a bouncy ball. He stopped searching and played with his ball for the rest of the hunt. I'm going to check out his section later and see what he missed. That real bacon treat is lying in wait for me!

Now it's time to go inside. Our company should be here soon, and I'm sure there's a scrap of ham waiting for me!

Wishing everyone a Happy, Blessed Easter Season!

Henry Pancake at the Library

Henry Pancake here about to head out to the city library. They are having a "read to your pet" day today. Mom wanted to check out a book so she decided to take Harley Bean and I in with her. Ranger D. stayed in the car with dad because he gets a little excited around people and pets. As soon as we entered the library, I noticed the slightly crabby looking librarian. She did not seem happy to see us. She accidentally dropped a book and Harley Bean latched on to it. The lady tugged at it, but HB would not let go. A page tore in the book and the librarian was really mad. Mom had to take the Bean back out to the car with Rangie and dad. She left the librarian in charge of me until she returned. My caretaker frowned at me, like something was my fault. I don't know what her name is, but I'll call her Madge because the first 3 letters describe her...MAD.

With a quick glance around the room, I noticed a calico cat on a leash, a nervous Nellie Chihuahua dog on a leash, and a cage with something in it. I have to move to get a better look at it … it's an iguana! Who wants to read to an iguana? There were also 2 girls in the children's section. The older one reading to the little one.

Mom came back to look for her book so she put my leash under a chair leg to keep me from roaming around. I'm sitting there minding my own business, when the older little girl came and freed me from the chair. She took me with her to read to me and the younger girl. I was happy to see she picked a book about puppies. How appropriate. I couldn't actually hear her reading, but when the younger girl laughed, I smiled too. The pictures were great seeing all the different dogs. The very last dog in the book was a Pug. The girls both laughed and showed me the picture of me in the book. Their smiling faces were such a treat to see. The girls got up to look for another book, but I thought they were leaving me stranded in the children's section. Would mom be able to find me? I started to get nervous so I let out a bark. Madge was in my face in less than 2 seconds. Her mouth was moving and she was shaking her finger at me. I looked down at the floor to let her know I was sorry and hoping she would leave, but mom heard the commotion and came to my rescue. She found her book and we were ready to leave. As we walked out the door, I wagged my tail at Madge hoping it would put her in a better mood. I doubt it did.

We stopped at a pet store on the way home. Ranger D., Harley Bean and I all got to pick out a new toy. I picked a fake book that squeaked. It reminded me of the little girls. On the ride home, I was thinking how cool it would be if someone would write a story about Henry Pancake. Only in my dreams, I guess.

Henry Pancake has a Picnic

Henry Pancake here with an exciting adventure to tell you. Mom and dad both had the day off. It was such a nice sunny day, so they decided to go on a picnic. Mom packed sandwiches for them and kibble for us pups (wish it was kibble for them and sandwiches for us). Ranger D., Harley Bean and I all hopped into the back seat and off we went.

We drove for a long time. Of course, when you share a back seat with Rangie and HB, 5 minutes could seem like a long time. Finally we stopped at a little secluded park. There was one other family there having a picnic also. We pups had to have our leashes on until the others left. I would stay put, but Rangie and the Bean don't understand personal space. Once the other family left, mom took our leashes off so we could explore the park. Of course, Ranger and Harley Bean took off running and rough housing all over. I tried to stay near mom and dad, but did wander off a little bit. There were so many pretty butterflies, bees and birds flying around. I also saw some pine cones and acorns on the ground. There were two deer off in the wooded area, but they stayed hidden. I came across another critter smelling the flowers. I recognized his black and white coloring as a skunk. Mom always said to stay away from skunks, but this one seemed nice. I called him Skip – Skip the skunk – has a nice ring to it. He and I roamed around together smelling all the wild flowers.

All of a sudden, I heard a rumbling noise. Sure enough, here comes Rangie and the Bean bounding towards us and not paying attention to where they're going. I quickly got out of their way, but Skippy didn't have a clue of what was happening. They plowed poor Skip over and sent him rolling down a hill. I think he was dazed for a minute, but once he stood up, he raised his tail and this awful smell filled the air. That got mom and dad's attention. They quickly gathered up us pups and the picnic stuff, loaded everything in the truck and off we went. There was a slight smell of Skip in the truck as we drove off. We had the rest of our picnic at our own patio in the comfort of our own yard.

I will always remember Skip…well, at least as long as his scent is in our truck. Now I see why we were warned to stay away from skunks, they don't know enough to stay out of Rangie and HB's way when they are rough housing!

Henry Pancake goes Camping

Hi folks! Henry Pancake here. Ranger D., Harley Bean and I have our harnesses on and are about to head out on a two-day vacation. A camping we will go! Mom and dad rented a small cottage at a campground a couple hours away from home. I've never been camping before, but it could be a fun time, as long as there is no dirt, bugs or horses involved. Dirt makes me get a bath, bugs bite and itch, and horses, well I don't have anything against them other than they are so much bigger than me. When they're near, I'm always worried about getting stepped on.

So we're off. After a long ride, we pull into this wooded area that has cottages and campers spread all over the place. Dad found our cottage, so we all got out to stretch our legs. First thing I noticed was the ground. We were walking in dirt! How am I supposed to keep myself clean for 2 days when I'm surrounded by dirt. I see a bath in my future. Rangie and the Bean started racing around like they always do. Rangie is a Chocolate Lab, they love water. He'll just go down to the lake and clean up. Apparently, the Bean doesn't care if she walks around looking like a mud pie.

Mom and dad had to go check in at the office, so they tied our leashes to a tree. We had to stay put until they got back. My next big discovery was bugs. No matter which way I faced, sitting or laying down, the darn bugs were buzzing around me. Rangie snapped at them with his mouth, but I don't think mom would be happy if I ate a bug, she keeps me on a strict kibble diet. Hope the bugs aren't in the biting mood or we'll be up scratching all night.

When mom and dad came back, they took us for a walk around the campground. There were a couple other pups with their families, and lots of kids that seemed to be enjoying themselves. All of a sudden, I stopped dead in my tracks. There, straight ahead of me was a horse! Everything I feared, happened. Mom could tell I was afraid, so she carried me over to meet the horse. His name was Chestnut, and he was very calm and polite. Mom even held me on his back and he took me for a short walk around. What a view! I could see three or four campsites all at once. I think Chestnut just became my new best friend.

Our weekend went by fast. We had a blast playing with the other campers. I didn't even mind the dirt. The fun we had was worth risking a bath when we got home. Harley had to have a bath before we left. Dad said there's no way that little mud pie was riding in his truck. Now our vacation was over and we had to head home. We said good-bye to our new friends and headed for the truck. The ride home was very quiet for dad. Three pups snoring in the back seat and mom sleeping in the front seat.

Thanks mom and dad for a great weekend. Don't forget to scrub behind my ears!

Henry Pancake Spends the Day With His Uncle

Hi Folks! Henry Pancake here with another exciting day in my life. Harley Bean and Ranger D. have appointments to get checked out at the vet. I had my checkup a while back so I get to spend time with my uncle, Frankie Doodle.

I really like Uncle Frank. He's almost my age, a bit chubbier and the only other pup I can actually pass up in a race. He moves a little slower, but he's always ready for an adventure. Today we laid around in the shade under a large Maple tree for hours. All of a sudden, a random leaf flew by, so we had to chase it. Surprisingly, it was my uncle who caught it! This comes as a surprise because Uncle Frank is vision impaired. Well, not quite impaired, but he only has one eye. When I want to annoy him, I call him Uncle Cyclops (haha). I can't tell you what he calls me, because remember, I'm deaf.

The pup next door (Ozzie) came over for a while. The 3 of us got along pretty good, but Ozzie's younger and has more energy than we do. Frank's mom would throw a ball and Ozzie would bring it back to me and Frank. That's my idea of fetch. Next Uncle Frank and I went for a ride and got our nails trimmed. It's not so bad when you go with a friend. We both got new bandanas and look very snappy.

When we got back to Frank's, a chipmunk ran in front of us. We both chased it, but we were both too slow. On our way back to the house, something hopped in front of us. I thought it was a weird looking bunny, but turns out it was a frog. Lucky for him, our nails were too short to harm him, so we let him hop away. My big mistake was nudging the little guy with my nose. It turns out I'm allergic to frogs. Just like Harley Bean and Ranger D., I ended up at the vet's office also. They had to get rabbie shots, and I had to get an allergy shot. When I got home, the 3 of us spent the evening comparing our vet stories. They seem to think it's funny that my face is swelled up. Maybe I'll ask Santa to bring them a frog for Christmas so they can see how much fun they are. But for now, our shots are making all of us pretty tired. G'night all.

Meet the Characters

Henry Pancake

Henry Pancake

Harley Bean

Henry Pancake & Harley Bean

Henry P. & Harley B.

Ranger D.

Ranger D

Titan

Ellie

Daisy

Frankie Doodle

Frankie Doodle & Ozzie

Harley B, Henry P, Rangie

Frankie Doodle

Ellie, Daisy, Titan

Happy Birthday Henry Pancake!

Henry Pancake's 11th Birthday

Henry Pancake here with another exciting day in my life.
Nothing exciting has happened recently so I am thinking back to about 6 months ago. It was my 11th birthday. Mom wanted to make the day special for me. She invited the neighbors over to help us celebrate. They consist of a mom, dad, 2 small children and 2 large dogs. I think the dogs are German Shepherds. They call them Butch and Bruno. The names are kinda scary, but the dogs look even scarier. Once we got to know them, we realized that they are pretty nice pups. They tend to ignore Harley Bean and me. Ranger D. is more their type of friend – big!

As a surprise for me, Mom blew up 11 balloons for us. Some just rolled around on the floor and some had strings attached. Harley Bean, the little stinker, ran full speed into the pile and popped 3 balloons right away. And then there were 8. As the day went on, the bigger dogs started playing with the balloons and 2 more popped. And then there were 6. There were still 2 balloons left with strings attached, so the small neighbor kids latched on to them. And then there were 4. Mom wanted to move the party outside, so we took some treats and cake outside, along with the rest of the balloons. Outside was fun, good idea Mom. The wind would float the balloons around. They almost looked magical. I was chasing one around the yard when it hit a spiked twig and popped. And then there were 3. Another floated into the bon fire. Didn't take long for that one to disappear. Now we are down to 2. Just before the neighbors went home, their little kids popped another balloon (on purpose I think). That leaves one left. Mom gathered up the balloon and the rest of the treats, and we headed back indoors. Dad turned the TV on to some sport show and got comfy on the sofa. I guess Mom wanted more attention because she started bouncing the last balloon in Dad's face. And then there were none! I'm surprised the balloons lasted as long as they did.

The day is done and the balloons are gone. Time to unwind and get our Jammies on. It was a good day for all of us. I'm sure we'll all sleep well tonight. I can't help but wonder how long 12 balloons will last next year.

Henry Pancake goes to the Vet

Henry Pancake here getting ready for a visit to the vet. I was walking around the yard just minding my own business, when I stumbled on to a bee's nest in the ground. Those little buggers were pretty mad that I invaded their space. First one came out and stung me, then a swarm started after me. I let out a loud yip and was running faster than I have ever ran. Unfortunately, I found out that a fast pug is no match for a mad bee. By the time dad rescued me, I had 4 bee stings around my popo area. It's strange that they could both sting and itch at the same time. My popo started to swell up (it's already the chubbiest part of me), so mom and dad took me to visit the vet.

By the time we reached the vet, I was pretty swelled up and lumpy. I looked like a partially deflated beach ball. The doctor quickly gave me an allergy shot to help with the swelling, pain and itch. They made me sit on the table for a while until the shot took effect, to make sure I didn't get dizzy or have any other symptoms from the shot. Note, the tables in a vet's office have a scale built into them, so all the while I was sitting there, my weight was on display for everyone to see. So embarrassing. After a while, I was feeling better. I stood up on the table and there, on the wall was a mirror. Oh my goodness. I am shaped like a pear. I have a pin head and a popo the size of New York City! Those bees really did a number on me. As we were leaving, the vet gave mom some medicine for me and then he put a cone on me so I won't aggravate my stings. Did you read that right? A CONE! How can a dignified pup like myself be seen in public looking like a lamp shade? I tried to keep my head down, but my cone scrapes the ground, so to make matters worse, I have to hold my head up high for all to see my face. This is one of the few times that I wish I could trade places with Harley Bean.

Once home, Rangie and the Bean started laughing and making fun of me. I went to the dog bed and laid down, but they kept running around me, prancing and wiggling their popo's. Finally, mom put a stop to it. I could see her shake her finger at them, and even though I couldn't hear her, I knew exactly what she was saying. "There will be no cone-shaming in this house. If you want to bully someone, go look in a mirror, it's not nice to make fun of someone's misfortune, etc." Thanks mom.

A week went by and I am now good as new. My cone hangs on a hook in our bedroom as a reminder to act smart or you could be the next one wearing it. I know I will be watching where I walk from now on. Maybe all bees could make their home somewhere else … like Georgia!

Henry Pancake visits his Cousins

Henry Pancake here. Today I'm thinking back to a weekend when mom and dad had to leave for a couple days so we pups had to be spread out. Ranger D. went to the neighbors to spend the weekend with Butch and Bruno. One of mom's coworkers has a small poodle, so she took Harley Bean to stay with them (she has no idea what she's in for). And lucky me, I got to go to my cousin's house. Titan, Ellie and Daisy, ready or not, here I come!

I was excited to see my cousins, and their yard is the coolest ever. There are so many neat smells, and there's also long grass and woods to explore. Titan and Daisy run so fast, I would need a jet pack to keep up with them. Ellie's a little slower, still faster than me, but willing to rest once in a while. I noticed the humans were really keeping an eye on me. That could be because the area is new to me, or because I am hearing impaired. Either way, I constantly felt eyes on me.

As I checked out the yard, I noticed these two turkeys following me (Gerald and Gina). Gina stayed back a little, but Gerald definitely needs a lesson in personal space. At times he was so close, his feathers ruffled my fur. Back off Gerald! I'm guessing the humans were tired of watching me so they stuck Gerald on my case. At one point, I tried to outrun him. That was a bad idea. Do you know how fast those huge birds can run? Faster than an elderly pug, that's for sure.

Next, I wandered along the edge of the wooded area. All of a sudden I stumbled on a chicken sitting on a nest of eggs. She did not welcome me to the area. She took off after me like a crazy bat. Cackling, pecking and chasing me out of her space. Holy smokes! Note to self: never ruffle the feathers of a mama hen.

Another lesson learned is to steer clear of the deer area at feeding time. They have an automatic deer feeder and when the corn sprays out, a small pug like myself could get crushed by the traffic. There are so many things to remember over here. No wonder Titan and Daisy just run all day. If they do get someone upset, no one can catch them anyway.

I have learned so much during my weekend with my cousins. I can't wait to see Rangie and the Bean to see if they had as much fun as I had. I doubt they did. Before I close this adventure, there is one more lesson I learned: stay clear of the swampy area or they'll insist on scrubbing you clean. Even my ears got scrubbed.

If there's ever a reason that I can't be home, I choose my cousin's home as the next best place.

Henry Pancake goes to the State Fair

Henry Pancake here with a great adventure to the State Fair. Mom and dad wanted to check out the Fair so they decided to take Harley Bean and me along for the day. Ranger D. had to stay behind because he's too young and nosy. He would be checking out all the exhibits, games, rides, food and mostly the other animals. Harley Bean and I just care about food!

Mom and dad borrowed a stroller from their friends to bring along for HB and I when we get tired. A PINK stroller. Pink, I tell you. A handsome, manly pug like myself being seen in public in a pink stroller. I should've stayed home with Rangie. I have a reputation to uphold.

The Fair was so cool. There was cotton candy, caramel apples, corn dogs, elephant ears, you name it, it was there. Harley and I being so close to the ground, found lots of treats. While mom and dad were looking at the exhibits and visiting with friends, we were stretching our leashes as far as possible to scour the ground for discarded food. What fun.

After 20 to 30 minutes of foraging for food, we started to feel a little full, bloated and miserable. We were glad the exhibits were close together so we didn't have to walk far, but standing around wasn't exactly a picnic either. After the exhibits, we headed to the animal barns. Oohhh, not only are we full of scrap food, now we get to smell animal stink. Pugs don't like stink, unless it comes from us.

Up and down the animal barns. One painful step at a time. Finally, mom and dad realized we were struggling so out came the pink stroller. Oh, the horror. But wait, there's a soft blanket for us to sit on and a nice support for our popo. This stroller may not have been such a bad idea after all. On to the games and rides we went. Checking out all the activities from the comfy of our seats.

On our way out of the Fair, we passed a Photo Booth. Mom and dad decided to get a picture so we'll always remember our first trip to the State Fair. And there we are – Harley Bean and I immortalized forever in a bright pink stroller! Maybe next year we'll go again and get a hat with a feather in it. Pink of course, to match our ride.

Henry Pancake goes to a Parade

Henry Pancake here with a very exciting day for us pups. Our town is celebrating their 100th birthday, so they are having a Centennial parade and we are going! Harley Bean, Ranger D. and I are all dressed up and ready to go. By all dressed up, I mean that mom put bandanas on us that say "100" on them. I sure hope nobody thinks that's my age.

We are all loaded up in the truck and off we go. Mom wanted to get their early to get a good spot along the parade path. Mission accomplished. We found a great spot for viewing and a nice grassy spot for us pups to lay in wait.

Harley Bean started jumping around and was excited, so I assume she heard the parade coming. Sure enough. It started out with the high school band marching and playing music, next came a float made by the senior class. This was followed by Boy Scouts and Little League players. Those youngsters had a long walk ahead of them. They should take turns pulling each other in a wagon. There were some classic cars in the lineup also. These got dad's attention. They also got our attention because they were tossing out pieces of candy to the spectators. We pups got all excited and tried to stretch our leashes to reach some, but mom wouldn't allow it. I'm not real fond of discipline. Next in the lineup came the horses. Prancing and marching with flowers in their hair. They got Rangie's attention. Dad had to hold his leash tight to keep him from joining the Lipizzaners (that's a horse that prances, in case you weren't aware). Along with the excitement of the parade, spectators also got to interact with clowns and people dressed up as Abe Lincoln, Tweety bird, Dopey the dwarf, Superman, and others that I didn't recognize. There was even someone dressed up like a dog. Can you imagine - there's real dogs here that could've been invited to march (not me, but Rangie). The fake dog didn't even have a bandana. Finally, the parade came to an end with a fire truck and police car to finish. It was definitely an exciting morning.

We stayed in town for a while and visited. I saw my Uncle Frank's neighbor, Ozzie, there. He had a bandana like ours on. We looked like band members. Mom and dad had a hot dog and ice cream while chatting with friends and neighbors. The day was supposed to end with fireworks, but we pups were getting pretty tired, so we all headed home. I think Harley Bean was faking being tired because she's afraid of fireworks. That works for me because they scare me too.

When I think of the town being 100 years old, it makes me feel like a youngster. I like that feeling. Now this youngster has had a busy day and his young bones (and mom) are telling him to go to bed. Sleep tight all!

Henry Pancake plays Hide and Seek

Henry Pancake here with another fun day in the great outdoors. It was a nice brisk Fall day with a slight chill in the air. My uncle, Frankie Doodle, was dropped off for a few hours. Mom said four dogs in the house would drive her to the loony bin. I don't know where that is, but she must not want to go because she sent us all outside. Since her and dad had to keep an eye on us, they decided it was a perfect time to rake leaves and catch up on some yard work. Us pups were busy chasing bunnies, chipmunks, wild leaves, and pretty much anything that moved. Of course, in our running around, we were also scattering the leaves that mom and dad just raked. They told us to find something else to keep us busy.

We put our heads together and decided a game of hide and seek might be fun and keep us out of trouble. We decided to stay hidden until mom and dad missed us and came searching. Ranger D. quickly ran to the edge of the woods and laid down. That sounds like an easy spot to find, but his brown color blended in with the dirt. If he keeps his eyes and mouth closed, he's pretty hard to see. Harley Bean crawled under the small tractor that dad was using to clean up the yard. Not a bad hiding spot, but I doubt she'll be able to sit still for very long. Next was Uncle Frank's turn. He just curled up next to a large decorative rock by the porch. The perfect spot for him. He blended in nicely. For my hiding place, I chose a large pile of leaves that mom and dad raked up. I crawled in the leaves and quietly laid down. This was pretty comfy. I could take a nap here. Now we just had to wait until mom and dad noticed we were gone.

As predicted, Harley Bean couldn't sit still very long. She crawled out from under the tractor and mom got pretty upset. Apparently, the tractor had a leak or something and the Bean had a stripe of grease down her back. While mom was upset about the grease, dad noticed that we were all missing. The hunt was on to find us. Dad knows Rangie pretty well, so he started looking by the woods. Ranger got so excited as dad got near that he jumped up and was spotted right away. Still two more to find. Next was Uncle Frank. He was so comfortable in his hiding place that he fell asleep. Mom and dad just followed the snoring sound and found him right away. Now they were stumped where to look for me. I let them search for a while, but I could tell mom was getting nervous. I poked my head out of the leaf pile and stayed like that until they found me. Mom and dad were laughing, us pups were jumping around and having fun. It was a good day for all of us.

Later, Uncle Frank went home and the Bean got her grease stripe cleaned up. Ranger D. was chewing on his toy, and I was sacked out on the couch. Mom placed a bright red leaf on my head as a reminder of my hiding spot. I love Fall!

Henry Pancake at the Haunted House

Henry Pancake here about to get the fright of my life. It was October and Halloween was approaching. Friends of mom and dad invited us over for a seasonal gathering. What we didn't realize was that their "seasonal gathering" included a trip to a haunted house. Mom and dad were a little worried, but didn't want to be rude and leave. So…in we go. Ranger D. is so young and goofy. He doesn't know how to be afraid. Harley Bean was a little scared so mom carried her. I tried to keep cool and look brave. I didn't want anyone to notice my teeth were chattering. Dad had Rangie on his leash. Mom was carrying the Bean and had me on my leash. I had to be brave.

First, a skeleton jumped out in front of us. Yikes! I almost swallowed my tongue. Next, I heard mom scream because she walked through a spider web. So glad I'm close to the ground. My bones are chilled. The fear is making me shed even more than usual. Onward we go. Our next big scare was a zombie emerging through a wall. I'm sure I peed a little when I saw him. Again, I'm thankful to be low to the ground. Hopefully he didn't spot me. Next was a witch stirring a pot of green gunk. She cackled and tried to lure us closer to her pot. I was visualizing cream of pug soup, and kept my distance. We were finally getting closer to the exit door. I put a little giddyup in my step to hurry us along. All of a sudden, two mean ghosts appeared out of nowhere and scared the (not pee) out of me. Definitely not like that ghost, Casper, that mom used to read to us. Mom and dad both gasped at the ghosts, and Harley Bean let out a bark. Ranger wanted to jump at them, but dad held him back. Lucky for Rangie or he could've been the third ghost.

Finally, we reached the exit. I never realized day light and sunshine were so wonderful. I believe I lost at least half my body weight just from fear shedding. Yes, that's a thing with pugs. I hope to never have this experience again. As a treat for finishing the haunted house, we were invited to pick a pumpkin from the pumpkin patch. Mom picked a medium sized bright orange one to take home. It looked nice on our front steps. That is until dad carved a bat figure into it. He put a light in the pumpkin so the bat would glow. Haven't we been frightened enough for one life time? Haunted houses must be created for the brave, fearless folks. Definitely not for pugs.

Henry Pancake in the Snow

Hi all, Henry Pancake here with another adventurous day in my life.

It is the middle of winter in the great state of Michigan. Activities this time of year include shoveling, plowing snow, snowmobiling, sledding, snow shoeing, and well, just about anything snow related. Our home is along a lake shore, and we have a large hill going down to the water (ice this time of year).

Mom and dad put their snowsuits on and got the snow tubes out of the garage. We all went outside to enjoy the fresh air. First, they built a life-size snowman complete with a top hat and broom. He looked like he came straight out of the Frosty The Snowman movie. Next we watched them glide down the snow hill and onto the frozen lake. Ranger D. chased after them running and tripping in the snow (what a goof). I stayed at the top of the hill shivering and freezing my toenails off. Harley Bean stayed by me, but she really wanted to go. Even her little mischief brain knew she'd never make it running down the hill. So she stayed, but was yipping and dancing around until finally dad decided to give her a ride.

She was quite a trooper on the way down. Dad held onto her, and the snow flying in her face didn't seem to bother her at all. Of course, she wasn't happy with just one ride. After a few more trips down the hill, mom decided to take the Bean with her. Mom didn't have a tight enough grip and Harley managed to break loose. Off the sled she went. Tumbling in the soft snow. Rolling, rolling, rolling and gathering more snow with each roll. When she finally stopped at the bottom of the hill, all you could see was 2 eyes, a nose, and 4 feet. The snow was so packed on, she couldn't shake it off. A real life pug popsicle! I was laughing so hard, I almost lost my footing and followed her. Thank goodness I was back far enough from the edge of the hill. Mom carried HB back up the hill and we all went inside so she could warm up. Rangie was a big help to her. He was licking/drinking the snow off of her. Dad started a fire in the fireplace and they roasted some marshmallows and had hot chocolate. I guess that's how humans warm up – they don't need Rangie licks.

While warming up, I noticed that if I sit on the back of the couch and look out the window, I can see the snow hill pretty good. That'll be my spot next time it's a sledding day. Snow can be fun, just not for this pug.

Merry Christmas!

Henry Pancake visits Santa

Henry Pancake here with Holiday Wishes for everybody. The Christmas Season is almost here. Dad went out in the woods and chopped a tree down for us to decorate. He brought it in the house and mom picked the perfect place for it. Mom got the box of ornaments, and the decorating has started. Dad was trying to get Ranger D. to help out. He would give Rangie an ornament and try to get him to put it on the tree. Of course, Rangie thought the ornaments were toys and tried to roll it around the house. Harley Bean and I are too short to help decorate, but when Rangie put the ornament on the floor, we joined in to chase it around the house. Mom was starting to get upset with us, so we had to calm down.

Finally, the tree was done. It looked magical. The shiny balls and ribbons looked great, but the star on top really made it look complete. As we all sat there admiring the tree, we saw a branch start to wiggle. Dad took a closer look, and out jumped a small chipmunk. Mom screamed and us pups got all excited. Ranger D. to the rescue. As fast as the little rodent jumped out, Rangie had him caught. Dad quickly opened the door so Rangie could bring him outside. A few bulbs fell off the tree and had to be replaced. It seemed like no big deal, but mom said no more real trees. It's artificial for us next year.

Next we went to the mall to visit Santa. It was supposed to be a special appearance by the jolly fellow to visit with pets, but there were also a few small children in line. When it was my turn, I marched right up to him. An elf picked me up and put me on Santa's lap. He patted my head, scratched my ears, and gave me a bag with 2 treats in it. I guess he could tell that I've been a good boy. Harley Bean was next. She was afraid to go up to him. Mom carried her to Santa and stayed right by her side the whole time. She growled a little when Santa pet her, but he still gave her a bag of treats. I bet she gets a bag of coal on Christmas. Finally, it was Rangie's turn. He sat on the floor next to Santa so he wouldn't hurt the jolly fella's legs. He's such a goof. He kept trying to lick Santa's face and hands. Santa gave him his treats in a hurry to send him on his way.

When we got home, mom let us have one of our treats. We had to save the other one for another day. I see why people enjoy the Christmas Season. It truly is the most wonderful time of the year.

On Christmas Eve, I got my jammies on and stood by the window watching for Santa. The jolly old fellow was sure to stop by soon.

Mom's wall plaque says it all: "May you never be too old to search the sky on Christmas Eve!"

Merry Christmas everyone! May all your wishes come true!

Made in the USA
Monee, IL
12 December 2024